The Playboy of the W

Study Guide 2020

CRACK THE COMPARATIVE #3

Amy Farrell

SCENE BY SCENE

WICKLOW, IRELAND

Scene by Scene
Wicklow, Ireland.
www.scenebyscene.ie

The Playboy of the Western World Study Guide 2020 by Amy Farrell.
ISBN 978-1-910949-79-5

Illustration © Askhat Gromov

Contents

About This Book

This book is a study guide for Leaving Certificate English students sitting their exam in 2020. It provides notes for the Comparative Study of *The Playboy of the Western World* by J.M. Synge.

There are notes and analysis of key moments for Cultural Context/Social Setting, Literary Genre, Theme/Issue (Relationships) and Hero, Heroine, Villain.

I have selected key moments to analyse for each comparative study mode. However, my choices are not definitive - any moment can be considered and explored for any mode. Feel free to consider other moments to add to your analysis for the comparative study.

The Playboy of the Western World by J. M. Synge

The play tells the story of Christy Mahon, who arrives in a remote village and receives respect and admiration for telling his tale of killing his father. However, his good fortune comes undone when his father follows him to this place and makes himself known.

Understanding the Mode
Cultural Context/Social Setting

Cultural Context/Social Setting refers to the world of the text. Think about social norms, beliefs, values and attitudes.

Consider the following questions to help you understand the Cultural Context/Social Setting of *The Playboy of the Western World*.

- What time and place is the story set in?

- What are the rules that characters live by?

- What guides characters' behaviour?

- What do characters fear?

- What do characters believe in – religion, power, love, family, wealth?

- What do characters prioritise – family, money, reputation?

- Who holds the power in this world?
  Who is powerless?

- How are the vulnerable members of society treated in this world?
  Are they protected or persecuted?

- Is this a supportive, loving world?

- Is this a harsh, threatening world?

- How does this world impact on characters' lives and relationships?

- How free are characters in this world?

- How controlled are characters in this world?
  Who controls them?
  Who has the power?
  Why do they have this power?
  Why are they obeyed/why are rules followed?

- What strikes you about the society of the text?

- Is this a sophisticated, civilised world?

- What is it like to live here?

- What is the world of this text like?

Notes on Cultural Context/Social Setting

The action of the play occurs in a **remote, rural Irish village in County Mayo in the early 1900s.** The centrepoint of the community is the shebeen, the public house where locals meet to drink.

The remote location adds a sense of **isolation** to the setting. Christy asks if police ever visit when he first arrives, saying it is over a week since he killed his father. The isolation of the place adds a sense of **lawlessness,** here they are beyond the reach of the law, at least until the villagers decide to respect it as the play ends.

The rural setting is clear when Christy speaks of digging spuds and walking the countryside, and when the Widow Quin bargains for a red cow, mountainy ram, dung and turbary rights. This is a **traditional farming community**, deep in the Irish countryside.

This traditional, remote setting adds to the excitement surrounding Christy's arrival and his terrible crime. **He is someone new, and dangerous, and as such, is very exciting and attractive to the locals.**

This is **a violent place,** where Christy's tale of murder wins him respect and admiration in the villagers' eyes and makes him more attractive to the local women. There is **something sinister and dark in the glamour the villagers see in Christy's crime.**

The **Widow Quin adds to the violence of this place** as she has committed a "**sneaky kind of murder**", where her husband died from blood poisoning after she hit him with a rusty pick. She describes herself as one who has "**buried her children and destroyed her man**", adding to the sense of darkness and **violence of this place**.

Marriage is very significant in this world. Shawn Keogh wishes to marry Pegeen, and is awaiting a church dispensation to do so. (This also demonstrates the significance and **power of the Church**). The marrying of cousins like this also shows how few people live here. There are not many potential matches available to young people, explaining perhaps why Pegeen would enter a 'bargain' like this with her cousin.

Pegeen herself is keen to marry Christy once she hears of his exploits. **In this world, marriage is the natural course for a romantic relationship to follow.**

There is a certain **coldness and cruelty in the society of this world.** Locals are **enthralled and thrilled to hear that Christy has murdered his father**, basking in the gory details of his crime. In fact, **his wrongdoing makes Christy more attractive here**, with Pegeen and the Widow Quin vying for his affections.

This cruelty is also apparent when Pegeen turns on Christy once she discovers that his father lives. Christy has lied to Pegeen, something that she cannot forgive him for, that reduces him horribly in her eyes, "And it's lies you told, letting on you had him slitted, and you nothing at all." In this world, **it is impossible for Christy to come back from such a lie**, and Pegeen **viciously punishes him**. She burns his leg, trying to make him release his hold on a table so that he can be dragged out for hanging. **There is savagery and brutality in how Christy is treated by the mob, and their willingness to judge and punish him. This is a harsh, unforgiving place, where people are willing to commit murder for feeling wronged, for being misled by an "ugly liar".**

The **spectre of the police and the law is worth noting at the play's end.** Pegeen refuses to "hang ... for a saucy liar, the like of you?" **The 'law' is used to justify violence and vigilante justice. The mob will punish**

Christy to protect themselves. Pegeen calls up the threat of the law, re-stating its importance now that Christy has fallen from favour.

In this world, characters' attitudes change quickly, and Pegeen is just as committed to the idea of Christy's destruction as she was to the idea of marrying him moments before. **Characters emerge as fickle and foolish**, throwing themselves wholeheartedly into one attitude, only to vehemently and violently reverse their outlook. This gives the impression of **an ignorant, judgemental society, with little wisdom or insight.**

Cultural Context/Social Setting Key Moments

Pegeen and Shawn's Conversation as the Play Begins

The setting of the shebeen sets the scene for the story. **This is a remote, isolated, rural place, deep in traditional Ireland**. The run-down shebeen is the local drinking place, a social hub in the community.

The opening dialogue between Pegeen Mike and Shawn Keogh, her cousin, gives an insight into the world of the text. **Pegeen and Shawn are related, and so need permission from the Church before they marry**. This shows they live in a **small community**, where **everyone is related**, while also showing the **significance and power of the Church.**

Pegeen mentions local crimes, giving a **violent backdrop** to this place, "Daneen Sullivan knocked the eye from the peeler", "Marcus Quin...got six months for maiming ewes".

Pegeen shows an **awareness of and fear of the law**. She asks Shawn what he will tell the peelers (police) about the man groaning in the ditch he was afraid to approach.

Pegeen is afraid to spend the night alone with her father away at the wake. This creates the sense that this is a **scary, threatening place**, while the **wake** reference tells us that this is a **traditional world where customs are followed**.

Christy's Crime is Seen as Bravery

The locals' attitude to violence and murder reveals a lot about the culture of this world. When the villagers learn that Christy has killed his father while digging spuds, they are impressed by his bravery. Rather than being shocked and appalled, they are excited by Christy's deed and admire him for it, "Bravery's a treasure in a lonesome place, and a lad would kill his father, I'm thinking, would face a foxy divil with a pitchfork on the flags of hell."

Their attitude to Christy reveals a lot about the attitudes of this world. **Violence is condoned and revelled in, there is little concern about the fact that what Christy did is wrong or illegal.** His crime is darkly interpreted as bravery, and **makes Christy more attractive and appealing to the villagers**, with Pegeen and Michael wanting Christy to stay and be their pot-boy.

There is a sense of a **warped moral code** at play, that a murderer should be celebrated and admired like this. There is **an absence of morality or justice** in the locals' outlook, "Now, by the grace of God, herself will be safe this night, with a man killed his father holding danger from the door."

The Widow Quin Arrives to Take Christy to Lodge With Her

The Widow Quin comes for Christy as **the priest says it is not fitting to have Christy lodging with an orphaned girl**. This shows both the **power and standing of the priest**, and also the **attitude towards women** in this world.

The priest has the power to decide this matter. Even though he has not set foot on stage, his authority is felt.

The view towards **women as being weaker beings**, in need of protection, is also clear. The Widow Quin comes to take Christy to lodge with her, to protect Pegeen from Christy, "There's great temptation in a man did slay his da".

It is also worth noting that Pegeen stands up to the Widow Quin and asserts herself here, demanding that Christy stays where he is, a battle that Pegeen wins. This shows that Pegeen is well able to assert and defend herself, suggesting that **women may be underestimated in this world**. Pegeen challenges the set way of doing things when it contradicts what she wants.

Christy Tells the Widow Quin his Tale of Murder

When Christy first tells the locals about killing his father, he says it was because he was "a dirty man, God forgive him, and he getting **old and crusty**, the way I couldn't put up with him at all." Christy's attitude here suggests a complete **absence of family duty or loyalty** and a **lack of respect for his father**, but also perhaps a desire to impress the villagers with his bravado.

Later, when he re-tells the story to the girls and Widow Quin, more is revealed about the world of the story. Christy describes digging spuds when his father told him to go to the priest and tell him he would wed the Widow Casey, "a walking terror". This highlights the **rural aspect** of the place as the men work the fields, but also the way **matches are calculated and made for material gain**, not for love or affection, "her hut to live in and her gold to drink." **This arranged match reminds us of Pegeen's betrothal to Shawn Keogh. This is a world without much emphasis on love, and a focus on what you can get.**

The **violence** of this place is also clear in Christy's attack on his father, "I hit a blow on the ridge of his skull, laid him out, and he split to the knob of his gullet." This violence and danger adds a certain glamour and attraction to Christy, with the women very impressed by his daring, "Well, you're a marvel!"

There is entertainment value in Christy's daring tale in this isolated place, "He tells it lovely."

Religious belief is an everyday part of this world, with Christy's arrival viewed by Susan as God's doing, "I'm thinking the Lord God sent him this road to make a second husband to the Widow Quin, and she with a great yearning to be wedded, though all dread her here." It is interesting that the Widow Quin is dreaded by all. A single woman, who has killed her husband, she adds to the sense of this **wild, lawless place**. It seems the **countryside is full of dangerous characters**.

Christy's Success at the Races

The **races are a big social event** in the village. Christy's success raises him in the locals' estimation, "He'd lick them if he was running races with a score itself." This is a **tight knit community**, and **Christy's participation and skill earns him respect and high social standing**.

The Widow Quin asks Mahon if his son was "a great hand at racing and lepping and licking the world." **His success as a sportsman casts him as something of a hero**, "They're cheering a young lad, the champion Playboy of the Western World."

Christy falls, remounts and recovers, asserting his athletic prowess, "He's fallen? He's mounted again! Faith, he's passing them all!" Christy is at the centre of the action, this little place is thrilled with the excitement of the races.

He is admired because of his racing success, "and the mountain girls hooshing him on!" Christy stands out as a winner in this place.

The Mob Turn on Christy

In the third act, when Mahon tells the crowd that he is Christy's father, the locals turn against their champion playboy.

There is an air of **merriment** and carnival around Mahon's appearance and Christy's changed circumstances that the locals revel in, betting on the row between Christy and Mahon, "Keep it up, the two of you. I'll back the old one. Now the playboy," and joining in "Pull a twist on his neck, and squeeze him so."

The **fickle nature of the villagers** is seen in the willingness of the crowd to turn on Christy, seeking his hanging. There is a **bloodthirsty** quality to the way Christy is treated, "Take him on from this or I'll set the young lads to destroy him here." The **cruelty and violence** of this place is apparent as Pegeen, who claimed to be in love with Christy moments before, scorches Christy's leg so that he can be dragged out for hanging, "Leave go now, young fellow, or I'll scorch your shins."

There is something **dark and sinister** about the ease with which Pegeen turns on Christy, inflicting pain on him. This shows that **this world is not just changeable, but wicked and cruel.**

Pegeen claims to fear the law and the repercussions the village will face for having Christy in their midst. She uses his crimes against him now, where once she admired what she saw as bravery, "Take him on from this, or the lot of us will be likely put on trial for his deed today."

The villagers are fickle and harsh in their treatment of Christy once he loses the glamour of being a murderer. **This is a dark, cruel place that is enthralled by violence.**

As the play ends, **the lasting impression of this remote place is that it is wild and violent, with the brutality of 'justice' and retribution always close to hand.**

Understanding the Mode
Literary Genre

Literary Genre focuses on the ways that texts tell their stories. When analysing Literary Genre, consider the choices the author makes in telling their story this way, and how this impacts on the reader's experience of the story. Think about aspects of narration such as the manner and style of narration, characterisation, setting, tension, literary techniques, etc.

Consider these questions when thinking about Literary Genre.

- How is this story told? (Who tells it? Where and when is it told? How is it structured? What does this add?)

- Why is the story told in this way?

- How does setting add to the story?

- Who is the main character (protagonist)?
  Do you like them? Why/why not?

- What are the protagonist's main characteristics?
  Are they an appealing character? Why/why not?

- How does this character change and develop during the course of the story? (character's arc) What causes these changes?
  Can you plot/chart these changes and developments?

- How does this character interact with other characters?

How does this add to the story?

- How are atmosphere and mood created?
  How do they add to the story?

- Is symbolism used to add to the storytelling?

- How do you respond to the narrative voice?

- Is this an exciting/engaging story? Why/why not?

- Does the author make good use of conflict/tension/suspense?

- What are your favourite moments in the story?
  What makes these moments stand out for you?

- How does this story make you feel?
  How does it cause you to feel this way?

- Is there just one plot or many plots?
  How do these relate to one another?

- What are the major tensions in the text?
  Are they resolved or not?

- Is this way of telling the story successful and enjoyable?

- Is the story humorous or tragic, romantic or realistic?

- To what genre does it belong?

Notes on Literary Genre

The Playboy of the Western World is a **play**, and this **performed dimension** of the narrative adds a lot to an audience's enjoyment of the text. The **story is presented as live action, by living actors, which adds to the emotional weight and impact of the story, as the audience can see and hear characters in front of them, and read their facial gestures and expressions.**

A very appealing aspect of the storytelling is the play's **dark humour.** Christy Mahon announces that he is a murderer, and is met with admiration and fascination by the local people. They are delighted to meet such a brave and daring man, and this unexpected response, as locals revel in **the glamour of Christy's crime, is darkly humorous, "There's a daring fellow."**

Shawn Keogh's character adds **humour** to the play also, as other characters mock him and make jokes at his expense, "It's true all girls are fond of courage and do hate the like of you." His constant mentions of marriage and pursuit of Pegeen adds to the humour at his expense.

The Widow Quin's constant scheming and manipulation also adds to the **dark entertainment.** She cuts a deal with Shawn that sees her benefitting nicely from marrying Christy, "A ewe's a small thing, but what would you give me if I did wed him and did save you so?" Her trickery and the easy way she manipulates Shawn makes her an entertaining, though self-interested character.

Christy's character is very engaging and entertaining; he is a likeable protagonist that adds charm and colour to the play. He appears

sensitive and shy at first, "I never left my own parish till Tuesday was
a week," and is transformed by the celebrity he earns from the label of
murderer.

Christy finds himself admired by the local women, an entirely new and
novel experience, and there is **humour** and **entertainment** in this. His
attitude to his father however, reveals **a darker side**, particularly when he
attempts to murder him a second time. The stage directions tell us *"he runs at
old Mahon with the loy, chases him out of the door... There is a noise outside, then
a yell, and dead silence for a moment."* Here we see Christy provoked to great
anger, attacking and attempting to kill his father in an effort to keep his
champion status with the local people. Christy's violence and anger here, and
when he tries to defend himself at the end of the play from the threatening
mob, shows another side to him, a violent, wild side.

There is something naive and vulnerable in Christy's misplaced belief
that killing his father will make amends and re-establish him as the village's
hero. After attacking his father for the second time he says, "I'm thinking,
from this out, Pegeen'll give me praises, the same as in the hours gone by."
He innocently believes that things will be as they were, and Pegeen will love
him again. **There is something very human and relatable in his wish
to make things better and go back to how they were. This mix of
sensitivity, violence and romance makes Christy a very compelling
lead character**, adding to the story's appeal.

The **love story** between Christy and Pegeen, threatened by the Widow
Quin's designs on Christy and the arrival of his father, adds **drama** and
excitement to the storyline. This **developing romance between Christy
and Pegeen is very engaging, and it makes the ending all the more
shocking and dark when Pegeen turns on him.**

Another aspect of the story that adds to the excitement, is that both

Christy and Pegeen have **additional love interests**. Pegeen has Shawn Keogh waiting on a dispensation from the bishop so that they might wed, while the Widow Quin makes it clear that she is interested in Christy. These **love rivals add a backdrop of conflict to Christy and Pegeen's relationship** that is interesting and exciting, engaging the audience.

The play is rich in conflict and confrontation, making it exciting, tense and engaging. **Mahon's return hangs over Christy** from the moment he spots what he thinks is his father's ghost approaching the shebeen. The Widow Quin does her best to send Mahon away, but he returns with dramatic consequences in the final act. **The return of Christy's father, and Christy's violent attempts to murder him a second time, are shocking and exciting, as is Pegeen's attempt to have Christy hanged in Act Three. Conflict adds immensely to the excitement of the story**, and to the audience's participation and enjoyment.

The play's ending is extremely tense and exciting, it is the climax that all the action has been building towards. Mahon, whose appearance has been threatening to ruin Christy, **confronts his son before being attacked a second time. Pegeen dramatically turns on Christy** when she learns his father lives, and for a time it appears he will be hanged. The **pacing** adds to the excitement here, as **events quickly spiral out of Christy's control**. Pegeen viciously scorches Christy's shin, trying to force him to let go of a table leg so that he can be dragged out for hanging. Christy's life is in real danger, the **audience are held in suspense** as to what will happen next.

It is Mahon's reappearance after Christy's second attack that ensures Christy's freedom, for now he is not a murderer again. Christy narrowly escapes a violent death, and leaves with his father.

This final section of the play is full of conflict, violence and excitement, and is very engaging for an audience. Christy leaving with his father may appear disappointing, considering the poor relationship the men share, but considering the situation, it is the only possible outcome. It is only when Christy and his father leave, and Shawn mentions marriage once more, that Pegeen softens and realises what she has lost.

Literary Genre Key Moments

Opening Scene

Pegeen and Shawn's conversation as the play opens establishes a sense of place and setting. The importance of the Church is established, as is Shawn's romantic interest in Pegeen, and the background references to crime and wrongdoing.

The **shebeen will be the focal point of the story**, all of the action will occur here, with the audience taking the place of guests or drinkers, privy to the shebeen's goings-on.

There is **humour in Shawn and Pegeen's relationship**, in his eagerness and her reluctance, which will be developed over the course of the play, "You're making mighty certain, Shawneen, that I'll wed you now."

Pegeen is fearful of the long night ahead, creating **a sense of threat and foreboding, but also, great anticipation for the audience**, "... I'm asking only what way I'll pass these twelve hours of dark, and not take my death with fear." There is a sense that this is a wild, dangerous place with hidden threat and menace.

Christy's Arrival

The locals are excited by Christy's claim that he is wanted by the police, eagerly asking what he has done, "If it's not stealing, it's maybe something big." There is **glamour to his criminal involvement, the locals are eager to hear all of the gory details**.

Interestingly, Pegeen does not believe Christy at first, saying he is too soft, and is only saying that he did something, "You did nothing at all." **Her confrontation is provocative, forcing Christy to declare himself a murderer while also foreshadowing the action of the play's ending,** "I killed my own poor father..." Then too, Pegeen will accuse Christy of being a liar for making false claims about his crime, and her anger will result in violence.

Christy's arrival and his backstory are exciting plot developments for the audience, engaging our curiosity and making us want to know more about his **character** and **story**.

The thrall that the villagers hold Christy in is also a noteworthy element of the narrative. **Christy's bloody crime confers hero status on him and makes him more interesting and attractive to the locals. This gives an insight into the setting and dark outlook of the villagers, while also adding to the story's humour.**

The Widow Quin's Arrival

The arrival of the Widow Quin brings **conflict** to the action. She challenges Pegeen, saying Christy should lodge with her, "There's great temptation in a man did slay his da, and we'd best be going, young fellow; so rise up and come with me." The **rivalry between the women adds tension and humour to the scene**, as each argues that Christy should stay with them. This makes the scene more interesting and exciting.

The Widow Quin also adds to the sense of a **violent setting** as she has, "buried her children and destroyed her man." Like Christy, she has a violent past, and like Christy, she walks free. **Her presence further continues the theme of violent killings.**

She also adds to the **feeling of the unpredictability** and wildness of the place. She suggests Christy should lodge with her, saying it is the priest's wish. She is interested in hearing more about Christy, and is not afraid to take on Pegeen. With the Widow Quin there is the sense that anything is a possibility.

She also adds to the developing relationship between Pegeen and Christy, trying to come between them. This adds **conflict** to the scene, and adds **excitement and anticipation regarding what will happen between Christy and Pegeen**. The Widow Quin's interest in Christy heightens his attractiveness, increasing both the element of conflict between the women, and the **humour** of the situation.

Mahon's Arrival

Mahon's arrival in the shebeen is an exciting, conflict-rich development. His appearance in Act II heralds a change in Christy's fortune, as the audience realises it is **only a matter of time before Mahon finds his murderous son**. This **adds tension** to the story, as we wait for Christy's father to seek his revenge.

In this regard, each of Mahon's moments on stage promises conflict to come. **His presence brings excitement and danger as the audience anticipates a showdown between him and Christy.** He has come looking for Christy, promising trouble, "I want to destroy him."

Mahon's arrival makes us question Christy's story and doubt his character, as we see for ourselves that he has not, in fact, killed his father. The audience wonders what will happen between Christy and Pegeen when the truth is discovered.

The Widow Quin tricks Mahon into continuing his search, "Gone over the hills to catch a coasting steamer to the north or south," **postponing the moment of confrontation, and so increasing the tension and suspense.** The audience knows this showdown cannot be much longer avoided, and **eagerly anticipates the conflict** that will ensue.

Pegeen Rejects Shawn Keogh

It is exciting as Pegeen challenges her father and rejects Shawn Keogh in favour of Christy. Shawn appears cowardly next to Christy, unprepared to challenge him for Pegeen's heart, "I'd liefer live a bachelor, simmering in passions to the end of time, than face a lepping savage the like of him." In rejecting Shawn, Pegeen goes against her father's wishes. This element of **confrontation** adds to the scene's **tension** and **excitement**, while furthering the **romantic plot line.**

When Shawn implores Pegeen to listen to him, Christy interrupts and threatens to murder him, taking up a loy before Shawn flees out the door, "Then I'll make you face the gallows or quit off from this." **This is an exciting moment, where Christy basks in his role of fierce murderer.**

Christy and Pegeen ask Michael to give them his blessing, which he does, "Bless us now, for I swear to God I'll wed him, and I'll not renege." This is **Christy as hero**, and **he revels in his role**.

However, this moment will be short-lived, as it directly precedes Christy's father's reappearance. **The admiration the villagers hold Christy in and his new found status will make his fall from grace more pronounced when his father appears**.

Christy Confronts his Father

Christy confronting his father, and the way the crowd viciously turn on him, is the play's **climax**. Christy's heroic tale of murder is exposed as a lie, and his father attempts to dominate him, ordering him to leave, "Rise up now to retribution, and come on with me." Pegeen turns on Christy when she discovers his father lives, adding to the scene's **drama** and **excitement**, "And it's lies you told, letting on you had him slitted, and you nothing at all."

Christy cannot quite believe his change of fortune and thinks if he kills his father he will reclaim the acclaim and admiration he enjoyed moments before. This spurs him into chasing his father and striking him with the loy, another grisly act of murder. Christy's second attempt on his father's life is a savage, brutal attack, a desperate attempt to regain control of a chaotic situation. **As with Christy's first attempt on his father's life, the violent action takes place off-stage**. Christy naively believes that, "from this out, Pegeen'll give me praises, the same as in the hours gone by." **The audience are eager to see whether Christy has regained favour with Pegeen, but matters continue to escalate out of his control as the tension mounts. Pegeen is resolute in her rejection of Christy, keen to see him undone for lying to her**.

This is a **tense, action-packed scene as violence escalates**. The **final outcome is unpredictable**, with Christy in real **danger** at the hands of the mob who decide to hang him to save themselves trouble from the police, "Pull a twist on his neck, and squeeze him so."

The violence is seen onstage as Pegeen burns Christy, and tries to have him hanged. Her feelings towards Chrsity have changed completely, she no longer loves him and wants him punished now that his story of murder has proved false, "Take him on from this or I'll set the young lads to destroy him here." **There is cruelty in her treatment of Christy, who moments before was the local hero.**

This scene is **exciting and dramatic** as Christy comes perilously close to losing his life. Just as Christy is being dragged out for hanging, the villagers notice old Mahon in their midst. Christy reacts in anger, "Are you coming to be killed a third time, or what ails you now?"

Mahon wants to take Christy with him to safety, "my son and myself will be going our own way, and we'll have great times from this out telling stories of the villainy of Mayo, and the fools is here."

Christy agrees to go, "like a gallant captain with his heathen slave." His time in the village has **altered Christy's perception of himself**, "you've turned me a likely gaffer in the end of all, the way I'll go romancing through a romping lifetime from this hour." **His time here has made him believe he is a winner and a champion.** While leaving with his father may feel like an unsatisfying ending for our protagonist, it is the only likely outcome as the locals have viciously turned on him and Pegeen has renounced her love. **Christy leaves with optimism for the future, while Pegeen returns to her monotonous life in the shebeen.**

Understanding the Mode
Theme/Issue – Relationships

Relationships has been selected as the theme/issue to explore in this text.
The theme of relationships can be applied to any relationship in a text and includes love, marriage, friendship and family bonds. When analysing this theme consider the complexities of relationships and the impact they have on characters' lives.

Consider the following questions to help you explore the theme of relationships.

- Are relationships generally negative or positive in the text?

- How well do characters communicate and express themselves to one another?

- Do characters trust each other?

- Do characters betray each other?

- Do you see conflict in the relationships in this text?

- Do characters love and respect one another?
  What makes them behave this way?

- How do relationships affect the storyline?

- How are relationships affected by the world of the text?

- Do the relationships in this text make life better or worse for characters?

  Do their relationships bring characters joy or sorrow?

- Are relationships complex and complicated?

  What makes them this way?

- Focus on a single significant relationship in the text – is it positive or negative?

  What makes it this way?

Notes on Theme/Issue - Relationships

Relationships in the play are flawed and destructive, despite the suggestion of love and marriage.

Christy has attempted to murder his father before the action of the play begins, he makes another attempt when the man appears close to the play's end. This **violence adds a very negative comment to the theme of relationships** in the play.

Christy's father mocks him and looks down on him, jeering him for being bad with women and commanding that he do as his father tells him. This further shows that their relationship is deeply flawed, as **Mahon treats his son like a wayward child.**

The potential and possibility of love falls short of delivering happiness to the play's characters. Although Pegeen and Christy's short-lived affair was full of promise as they looked lovingly to their future together, she **turns on him** as soon as she learns that his father lives, angered that she has been lied to, "And to think of the coaxing glory we had given him, and he after doing nothing but hitting a soft blow and chasing northward in a sweat of fear." She wants Christy hanged for his crime lest the villagers be implicated in it, "And leave us to hang, is it, for a saucy liar, the like of you?" Pegeen brutally burns Christy in an attempt to manoeuvre him out the door. **Her cruelty towards Christy, and the speed with which she turns on him, makes the audience consider whether there was ever real substance or emotion to their relationship at all**.

Relationships between minor characters are also troubled and flawed. Shawn Keogh proclaims to be in love with Pegeen, but she drops him without a second thought in favour of Christy. **This shows us how little Pegeen's promise to marry him is worth**.

Shawn also fails to challenge Christy for Pegeen's heart, "I'd be afeared to be jealous of a man did slay his da." He gives up easily, making us question the strength of his commitment to Pegeen.

Similarly, the Widow Quin adds a negative note to this theme. Her **bargaining and negotiating** with Shawn about marrying Christy **removes the idea of love from these relationships**. She offers to marry Christy while bargaining with Shawn Keogh, her **motivation is mercenary, not emotional.**

The damaged, flawed aspects of these relationships, the violence and anger characters show towards each other, coupled with characters' calculating and self-interested attitudes to marriage, shows a consistently negative portrayal of relationships in this text.

Even as Christy leaves with his father at the play's end, he adopts the position of master in their relationship. **Characters do not love and value others, but use them for their own ends.**

Theme/Issue-Relationships Key Moments

The Play's Opening

Pegeen and Shawn have made "**a good bargain" to marry**, waiting on a "dispensation from the bishops." The 'bargain' element here shows this is a **calculated affair**, not motivated by love or passion. **Marriage is something to be negotiated and arranged, it is not necessarily a union entered into because of love**.

The need for a special dispensation highlights something unusual about this union. Pegeen and Shawn are cousins, so special permission is required. Once again this appears as an arranged affair. It is not motivated by love.

Shawn appears more eager than Pegeen to enter this marriage. This is an **unbalanced, one-sided relationship** that Pegeen may feel she must enter as she has little other choice. There is the sense that **Pegeen may be settling for this marriage** as she has no other romantic prospects or options available to her. **It is a marriage of necessity, not of love**.

Christy's Attraction

Once Christy reveals that he has killed his father, he becomes much more interesting and attractive to the locals. Pegeen asks her father to make him the pot-boy so she will no longer have to be scared. Christy's **violent deed is interpreted as proof of bravery, making him very attractive** and exciting to the villagers, "herself will be safe this night, with a man killed his father holding danger from the door." Pegeen is keen to talk to Christy and hear all about his life and crime. **His father's murder makes him glamorous, exciting and brave in Pegeen's eyes**. She finds it hard to believe that he does not have a girlfriend already.

This suggests that traits the villagers find appealing are in reality quite dark and negative. It is not only Pegeen, but also the Widow Quin and the local girls who are **drawn to Christy because of the murder** he has committed, "That's the man killed his father." This adds a **negative aspect to the theme of relationships, that such violence and wrongdoing should inspire admiration and attraction.**

The fact that Christy is so readily accepted by the villagers, and Pegeen in particular when he reveals that he has killed his father, demonstrates **negative relationships** in the text. **No-one suggests that killing one's father is a bad thing, suggesting a lack of love in family relationships. Pegeen wants to be with Christy because she believes he is a murderer. Perhaps this is a questionable start to a firm relationship, with Pegeen caught up in excitement rather than real emotional feeling.**

Christy Tells the Widow Quin his Story of Murder

Christy tells the Widow Quin the story of how he murdered his father. Christy's story of murder reveals a **negative, flawed relationship** with his father. He describes **arguing** with his father who wanted Christy to marry an older woman, a "walking terror" for her hut and gold. **His father's motivation for Christy marrying is greed and personal gain**, he does not care whether his son wants to marry. This shows the **calculated, self-interested side to relationships in this place.**

Their **argument is full of threats**, "I'll flatten you out like a crawling beast", and **violence**, "I hit a blow on the ridge of his skull", revealing **a relationship full of conflict, antagonism and aggression.**

It is also worth noting that Christy shows **no sign of remorse** for his actions. He is not upset by his violent deed, nor does he mourn or grieve for his father. This suggests a **coldness** and distance between them, and a **lack of a meaningful family bond.** Christy delights in his tale of murder, "He tells it lovely," and is **unmoved by what he has done,** unaffected it seems by ending his father's life.

It is also important to note the attention and admiration the girls and Widow Quin give to Christy here, "Well, you're a marvel! Oh God bless you! You're the lad, surely!" **Christy's violent deed makes him interesting and attractive**, earning him this female attention, "I'm thinking the Lord God sent him this road to make a second husband to the Widow Quin."

Christy's appeal suggests something warped or amiss in the relationships of this text, where such a violent crime is celebrated and seen to make the perpetrator so attractive. No one questions the character of a man who would kill his own father, suggesting a coldness or cruelty in the relationships of this world.

Mahon Comes to the Shebeen

When Mahon arrives searching for his son, **he appears to hate Christy just as much as Christy hates him**, describing him as "an ugly young steeler with a murderous gob on him" and "a dirty stuttering lout". Clearly, **Christy and his father have a very negative, difficult relationship.** Mahon's low opinion of Christy is evident, as are his **violent intentions** towards his son, "I want to destroy him for breaking the head on me with the clout of a loy." Mahon's intention is to pay Christy back for the violent assault he has suffered. **Vengeance is his motive, showing the bad feeling between these characters.**

Mahon mocks and insults Christy in his description of him to the Widow Quin, calling him "the laughing joke of every female woman where four baronies meet". **Mahon thinks little of Christy, and his words show no fondness or affection for him.**

The Widow Quin manages to send Mahon on his way by telling him that she has seen his son pass by. In his eagerness to catch Christy and get his **revenge**, Mahon leaves. When he is gone, Christy's first thoughts are not of his father, but rather, what Pegeen will say when she discovers the truth. Christy is angry with his father for "letting on he was dead" and "following after me like an old weasel". There is **no sorrow or pity here, no regret** for what he has done, just **rage** that his father has followed him like this.

Pegeen and Christy Talk of Marriage

After Christy's great success at the races, **Pegeen and Christy appear to be smitten with one another.** Christy boldly asks Pegeen to "promise that you'll wed me in a fortnight", as **his heart is set on Pegeen.**

She is just as **keen to marry immediately** and "not wait at all". They are **caught up in the idea of being together. Pegeen remarks on the change that Christy has made in her**, "to think it's me talking sweetly, Christy Mahon, and I the fright of seven townlands for my biting tongue."

Pegeen asserts herself, telling her father that she will marry Christy. Michael (her father) is taken aback, concerned that Pegeen would be "making him a son to me, and he wet and crusted with his father's blood". Pegeen is not dissuaded by her father, holding firm in her intention to marry Christy. She **defiantly commits to Christy, rejecting her planned match** with Shawn Keogh, "He's missed his nick of time, for it's that lad, Christy Mahon, that I'm wedding now." Pegeen is determined to marry

Christy, the object of her heart's desire. **Their relationship is still very new, but shows commitment, passion and possibility, and disregard for what others may say or think.**

Christy Confronts his Father

Just as Christy and Pegeen receive Michael's blessing for their wedding, Mahon arrives on stage. He **orders Christy to leave with him, maddening Christy** who turns to the crowd for support that does not materialise.

Despite his earlier attack on him, **Christy's father is unafraid of his son**, beating him and telling him what to do. This gives an insight into their relationship; **it is clear that it is Christy's father who is in charge here.**

Mahon's arrival destroys Christy's relationship with Pegeen, as it transforms him into a liar in her eyes, "...I'm hard set to think you're the one I'm after lacing in my heart-strings half an hour gone by." **She instantly loses all admiration for, and interest in Christy, and is vicious and cruel towards him.** Pegeen is especially cutting in telling Mahon to take Christy before she tells the "young lads to destroy him here." **Her reaction to Christy's boastful claims of murder being proven false is violent anger.** It seems Pegeen is more concerned about being lied to than the fact that Mahon still lives, showing a self-centred, self-concerned outlook, "And it's lies you told, letting on you had him slitted, and you nothing at all."

Christy, overcome with emotion, tries to murder his father a second time. This **indicates how little he thinks of his father, that he could attempt to end his life once more.** It also **shows how much Christy wants to be with Pegeen, that he takes this drastic action to try to make amends and make things between them as they were,** "I'm thinking, from this out, Pegeen'll give me praises, the same as in the hours gone by."

Christy's violent outburst fails in winning back Pegeen, and she scorches his shin to help the others drag him out for hanging. **The speed with which Pegeen has turned on Christy, and the cold way she speaks to him, forces us to question whether there was ever any real substance or value to their relationship,** "he an ugly liar was playing off the hero, and the fright of men."

Surprisingly, Christy leaves with his father. Despite his attacks on the man, and the **obvious flaws in their relationship**, they are **united as the play ends**. The events in the village have reconciled them to some degree, "my son and myself will be going our own way." **Christy declares that he will be his father's master from now on** before they leave, suggesting he wants to have the upper hand in their relationship from now on, "for I'm master of all fights from now."

Understanding the Mode
Hero, Heroine, Villain
(Ordinary Level)

'Hero, Heroine, Villain' refers to studying central characters (protagonists/antagonists).
Their traits, values, etc. and their ability to deal with conflict, challenges, obstacles, etc. should be considered.
Think about a character's personality, their behaviour, what you like and dislike about them, etc.

Focus on a single character as you consider the following questions:

- Is this character a 'good' main character?
  Are they interesting?
  Are they likeable?
  Do you care about what happens to them? Why/why not?

- What problems and difficulties do they face?
  Do they find facing these problems easy?

- What does this character struggle with?

- What are they good at?

- What makes this character happy?

- Do you feel sorry for this character at any point? Why/why not?

- What sort of life has this character had?
  How has this affected them?

- Describe this character's personality.

- What is important to this character?

- If you had a conversation with this character, what would you talk about?
  What advice would you offer them?
  Do you think they would be an easy person to talk to about their problems? Why/why not?

- Do you like this character?
  What makes you feel this way?

Notes on Hero, Heroine, Villain (Ordinary Level)

Christy Mahon, the play's protagonist, is a very interesting character. He is lively and **entertaining** to watch and **brags of murdering his father**, relishing the telling of his tale. The way he announces himself as a murderer suggests he is **a naive character**, to reveal so much to strangers, "I killed my poor father." This **innocent** streak is also seen in his antics with the local women. He revels in their attention, delighting in their interest in him. It seems **he does not have much experience with women**, and is flattered by their interest in him and his stories of murder, "It's a long story; you'd be destroyed listening."

With Pegeen, he appears as a **hopeful**, optimistic character, romantically looking forward to their life together, "I'll have great times if I win the crowning prize I'm seeking now, and that's your promise that you'll wed me in a fortnight." Despite his lack of experience with women, he commits wholeheartedly to the idea of a romantic future with Pegeen.

Christy's success at the races makes him appealing to the locals. Christy is lucky and athletic, qualities admired by the villagers, that add to his status of murderer.

There is also a darker side to Christy Mahon. His tale of murdering his father shows **violence, irreverence and immorality**. The locals describe him as **daring and brave** for committing such a feat, but the audience needs to consider the **reality of Christy's crime**, striking down his own father as he worked the fields, "I hit him a blow on the ridge of his skull, laid him out, and he split to the knob of his gullet."

It is also significant that when his father turns up in the village, Christy is **enraged** by his presence and attempts to kill him a second time, out of self interest and an attempt to preserve his love affair with Pegeen, "She'll wed me surely, and I a proven hero in the end of all."

This **anger and violence highlights the darker, dangerous side of Christy's personality**. Indeed, as the mob try to drag Christy out they witness his violent anger, "... let the lot of you be wary, for if I've to face the gallows, I'll have a gay march down, I tell you, and shed the blood of some of you before I die."

Christy has come to believe in the mythology the villagers have created for him. It is this daring, brave side we see at the play's end when Christy escapes the village as his father's master, "... you've turned me a likely gaffer in the end of all, the way I'll go romancing through a romping lifetime from this hour to the dawning of the Judgement Day."

Hero, Heroine, Villain Key Moments

Christy's Arrival

Christy is **polite and courteous** when he arrives in the shebeen. He asks about police visiting the place, alerting those gathered to his wrongdoing. He **enjoys the locals taking interest in his crime**, and **brags** about it,

"I'm not calling to mind any person, gentle, simple, judge or jury, did the like of me."

Pegeen is not convinced by him, "A soft lad the like of you wouldn't slit the wind pipe of a screeching sow." Clearly, **Christy does not strike Pegeen as the violent type.** She threatens to hit him with her broom, and he tells her what he has done out of fear, "Don't strike me. I killed my poor father..."

Our first impression is one of a **shy, polite** young man. The news of his father's murder suggests a **hidden side to his personality**.

Christy's Dark Side

Christy appears to be a **gentle, meek** character when he arrives, but he goes on to tell Pegeen that he has a **dark, hidden side**, "Up to the day I killed my father, there wasn't a person in Ireland knew the kind I was...". He plainly admits to having a hidden, **violent side**, which is proven by his attack on his father. However, Pegeen sees this as a very **attractive** quality, "...The girls were giving you heed...".

Christy is very **honest**, and tells Pegeen that he is not popular with girls. He appears as a **chatty character**, who **delights in the attention his dark deed brings him.**

Christy's Reaction to His Father's Arrival

Christy is afraid when he sees his father approaching the shebeen, "Where'll I hide my poor body from that ghost of hell?" He is **terrified**, thinking he sees the ghost of his murdered father coming for him. His reaction here suggests **he is a softer character than the brave, fierce murderer he has claimed to be. When his father comes in, Christy hides** behind the door, and stays there while the Widow Quin speaks with his father.

When she finally sends him on his way, Christy re-emerges and immediately thinks of how his father's appearance will impact on his blossoming romance with Pegeen, "What'll Pegeen say when she hears that story?" He is **selfish** here, totally unconcerned about his father.

He asks the Widow Quin to help him win Pegeen, "Will you swear to aid and save me, for the love of Christ?" **He seeks the widow's help, rather than relying on himself. His inability to face his father, or help himself regarding Pegeen, shows a lack of strength and fortitude.**

Winning at the Races

Christy's success at the races paints him as **a local hero, young and athletic, blessed with skill and good luck**, "He's fallen? He's mounted again! Faith, he's passing them all!"

He is **celebrated by the locals**, "Good jumper! Grand lepper! Darlint boy!" and **revels in his success, bragging about his father's murder**, "Thank you kindly, the lot of you. But you'd say it was little only I did this day if you'd seen me a while since striking my one single blow." **Christy enjoys the attention and praise he is receiving, and it makes him bolder and braver so that he proposes to Pegeen.** He is now a **confident character**, convinced of himself because of his reception and success in the village.

It is also worth considering the fact that **Christy knows his father is**

alive, yet he continues to boast of his murder. This suggests a failure to think things through, or perhaps a hopeless optimism.

Christy Plans to Marry Pegeen

Following his great success at the races, Christy proposes to Pegeen, "I'll have great times if I win the crowning prize I'm seeking now, and that's your promise that you'll wed me in a fortnight". **He is enthusiastic and romantic**, imagining his future with Pegeen, "squeezing kisses on your puckered lips". He is very **happy** to have found her.

Pegeen's father, Michael, plans for her to marry Shawn Keogh, and Christy shows daring in opposing this match. He threatens Shawn, "...I'll maybe add a murder to my deeds today", who is too afraid to fight him. Christy is **confident** and **sure of himself**, telling Michael that he will bring luck to the house, "it'll be good for any to have me in the house." He believes in the version of himself that the villagers do, buying into this mythology.

Christy Faces his Father

Christy's first reaction on seeing his father in the final act is to lie and deny that it is really him, "He's not my father. He's a raving maniac would scare the world."

When the crowd call him a liar for this, he denies it, **angrily calling his father the liar**, "It's himself was a liar, lying stretched out with an open head on him, letting on he was dead." **Both Christy's denial here, and calling his father a liar, are childish responses**.

He **acts in desperation when he violently attacks his father**, trying to restore his relationship with Pegeen and good standing in the village, "I'm thinking, from this out, Pegeen'll give me praises, the same as in the hours gone by." **His belief that things will go back to how they were before his father's arrival is childish and naive. He does not grasp at first that things have changed for good between him and Pegeen.** There is something innocent and vulnerable in Christy's assertion that "I'll not leave Pegeen Mike." Christy does not realise that their relationship is over, that she has turned on him completely, until she slips the hangman's noose over his head.

When the crowd turn on him, wanting to see him hanged, **he threatens them with whatever violence he can** inflict before they kill him, showing **spirit and strength of character in the face of danger.**

As the play closes, the audience is left with the impression that there are **two sides to Christy's character. He is both the charming talker, and the violent character he has claimed to be.**